CHARLES
LECLERC

100% UNOFFICIAL

Published 2024 by Macmillan Children's Books
an imprint of Pan Macmillan
The Smithson, 6 Briset Street, London EC1M 5NR
EU representative: Macmillan Publishers Ireland Ltd, 1st Floor,
The Liffey Trust Centre, 117–126 Sheriff Street Upper
Dublin 1, D01 YC43
Associated companies throughout the world
www.panmacmillan.com

ISBN 978-1-0350-4394-1

Text copyright © Maurice Hamilton 2024
Illustrations copyright © Cat Sims 2024

1 3 5 7 9 8 6 4 2

A CIP catalogue record for this book is available from the British Library.

Printed and bound by CPI Group (UK) Ltd, Croydon CR0 4YY

MIX
Paper | Supporting
responsible forestry
FSC® C116313

All facts correct at time of printing.

RACING LEGENDS

16 **CHARLES**

LECLERC

Maurice Hamilton

Illustrated by Cat Sims

MACMILLAN CHILDREN'S BOOKS

CONTENTS

Formula 1 is one of the **most exciting** sports in the world.

It is **noisy, colourful** – and VERY, VERY **FAST!**

Formula 1 cars can reach speeds of up to **320 kmh (200 mph).** That's three times faster than the 113-kmh (70-mph) speed limit on motorways, the fastest roads you can use in the UK.

The F1 cars race side-by-side at these **unbelievable speeds.**

It takes very special and very **brave drivers** to do this in these **incredible** machines.

That's why the twenty F1 drivers are the **best in the world.** They come from all sorts of countries, and race all around the globe.

I love watching F1. I've been SO lucky to attend more than 500 Grands Prix around the world!

Hi, my name is Maurice

These drivers compete against each other in races known as **Grands Prix** (which means 'Great Prize' in French!).

And it certainly is a Great Prize – champion teams win millions of pounds!

They drive for ten F1 teams, with two drivers in each of these **top** teams.

Ferrari is the most famous. The Italian team has been racing **for more than 75 years.**

The Mercedes and Red Bull teams have won the most races in the past ten years. Both these teams are based in England.

There are more than twenty Grands Prix held from March to November around the world.

Each race track is different. Some are on city streets – like in Monte Carlo, Baku in Azerbaijan or Las Vegas in the United States. Once the Grand Prix has finished, the crash barriers and grandstands are removed and the normal traffic – cars, buses, vans – returns to the streets.

Other Grands Prix are on permanent circuits built for racing – like Silverstone in England, Suzuka in Japan or Monza in Italy.

The length of the laps is also different. Monaco is the shortest at 3.34 km (2.07 miles). Spa in Belgium is the longest at 7 km (4.35 miles).

Each race lasts for an hour and a half – sometimes longer.

The winner of each race receives twenty-five championship points. Points are awarded down to 10th place like this:

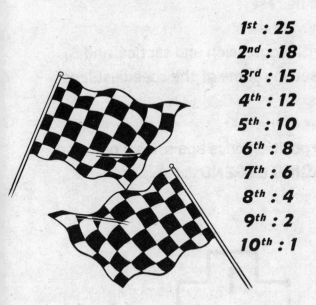

1st : 25
2nd : 18
3rd : 15
4th : 12
5th : 10
6th : 8
7th : 6
8th : 4
9th : 2
10th : 1

After the last race of the year, the driver with the most points becomes **World Champion!**

This is the greatest honour in motor racing. The World Champion is the BEST driver.

And bursting onto the F1 scene with **SPEED** and **STYLE** is one special driver . . .

He is from the home of motor racing itself and was born to be fast . . .

He drives with aggression and tactics, and is known for setting some of the speediest laps on record . . .

Taking pole position once again, it's a new and exciting **RACING LEGEND . . .**

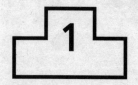

CHARLES LECLERC!

WHO IS CHARLES LECLERC?

Charles Leclerc is one of the **most exciting** drivers to have arrived in F1 in recent years.

He comes from a family of racers. His dad, Herve, used to race in Formula 3.

Charles's younger brother, Arthur, races in Formula 2 – which is the next level down from Formula 1.

Their elder brother, Lorenzo, was best friends with the Formula 1 driver, **Jules Bianchi.**

Jules became Charles's godfather. Very sadly, he died after an accident during the 2014 Japanese Grand Prix.

Because he was brought up in Monaco, which is surrounded by France, with Italy very close, Charles speaks **French** and **Italian,** as well as **English.**

Charles began racing karts when he was **seven years old** and was soon winning many trophies and championships.

In the 2013 World Karting Championship, Charles finished second – behind **Max Verstappen,** who Charles would soon be racing against in F1.

Max Verstappen has won over fifty Grands Prix in his legendary career.

Like other **RACING LEGENDS,** Charles would move from karts into small racing cars.

In 2014, he finished runner-up in the Formula Renault championship before stepping up to Formula 3 in 2015 and showing fantastic promise.

He was asked to join the **Ferrari Driver Academy** and become one of Ferrari's test drivers.

 8

 9

CHARLES'S LEGENDARY STATS

Coordination:	10/10
Control:	10/10
Precision:	9/10
Balance:	10/10
Wet Weather Skills:	9/10

Acceleration:	**9/10**
Fitness:	**9/10**
Staying calm:	**7/10**
Split-second decisions:	**9/10**
Strategy:	**8/10**

A FAMILY
OF RACERS

Monaco is known as a city-state. It's a tiny place. About 40,000 people live there. You

could fit all of those people into **one football stadium!**

One third of the Monaco population are **millionaires.** Most were not born or brought up in Monaco.

Charles Leclerc had a very happy childhood in La Condamine, a modest area by Monaco's port.

The bus taking him to school each day would drive on some of the streets used once a year for the Monaco Grand Prix.

Charles was very good at mathematics and speaking languages. When he became a Grand Prix driver, his school hung a picture of Charles on the wall of his old classroom as an example of what is possible if you work hard!

A friend of Charles's family had an apartment which overlooked the race track. Charles watched the Grand Prix from there when he was aged four. He loved the excitement, the noise – and the racing!

His father, Herve, took Charles to a kart track, across the border in France.

Even though he was only four and very small, Charles loved the thrill of sitting behind the wheel of a kart. This was when he decided he wanted to one day become a racing driver.

This kart track was looked after by Herve's best friend, Philippe Bianchi.

Philippe had two sons, Jules and Tom. Jules was eight years older than Charles and raced karts. He was very fast. Jules would become Charles's mentor, giving advice as Charles grew up and began to race karts.

VROOOM

GOING
KART RACING

Charles was only seven years old when he began to race karts. Jules Bianchi would sometimes work as a mechanic on Charles's kart. They became very close.

They had a lot of fun at the kart track in France. Jules was very proud when Charles won a local karting championship. Charles was so good, he won the championship **four years in a row!**

As Charles grew older, he moved onto the bigger, more important championships and became **French Cadet Champion in 2009.** The Cadet class is for boys and girls aged between eight and twelve.

The following year, Charles moved up to the CIK-FIA World Cup and raced against **Max**

16

Verstappen and **Esteban Ocon,** two drivers he would later compete with in Formula 1. But that seemed a long way off at the time.

In 2010, all of these young drivers were keen to prove they were the best and move into single-seater racing cars.

 17

The problem was, Mr and Mrs Leclerc did not have enough money to support all three of their sons in racing. Lorenzo stopped racing to allow the family to support Charles – who Lorenzo knew was even faster than he was. That was a generous thing to do. But the family still needed support.

Jules Bianchi's dad introduced Charles to some influential people in motor racing who agreed to try and help. But, first, Charles had to prove he was worth their support by continuing to win kart races.

In 2011, Charles **won a World Karting Championship** in a category for thirteen to fifteen-year-olds – and beat Verstappen! The next year, Max and Charles collided while fighting for the championship.

In 2013, they were neck and neck again! This time, Max won the championship and Charles finished a very close second. Now it was time for them both to move onto single-seater racing cars.

THE NEXT STEP

In 2014, the time was right for Charles to take on the challenge of racing in Formula Renault. Lewis Hamilton and many other future F1 drivers had taken their first steps in car racing with Formula Renault.

Formula Renault cars are basically very, very simple – but fast! – Formula 1 cars. When it's dry, Formula Renault cars use 'slicks' – just like F1 cars. Slick tyres have no treads – which you need for getting rid of water on the road when it's wet. Slicks give lots of grip and allow you to corner faster on a dry surface.

Charles loved Formula Renault and won two races and finished on the podium lots of times. He won a Formula Renault Junior

F1

F2

F3

Championship for new drivers in 2014.

In 2015, Charles took the next step to more powerful Formula 3 cars. He drove for **Van Amersfoort Racing,** the same team Verstappen had raced with the year before!

GO-KART

Charles made a big impression on his first weekend of F3 at Silverstone. There were three F3 races that weekend. Charles was in pole position for two of them and won the third!

Max had finished third in the 2014 F3 championship. Charles, after leading the 2015 championship at one stage, eventually finished fourth and was **Rookie of the Year** – the prize given to the best newcomer.

ONTO GP3

Charles had been so impressive in 2015 that he was invited to the **Ferrari Driver Academy.** This is the programme that allows the Ferrari team to train the young drivers they think might be good enough one day to become Formula 1 stars.

The Ferrari Driver Academy coaches drivers and helps with their fitness.

This came at a good time for Charles because he had also been chosen to race in GP3 with ART, one of the top teams.

GP3 races take place on the same weekend as Grands Prix. This means young drivers are being watched by the important managers in Formula 1 as they look out for drivers they might one day sign for their teams.

Charles **won his very first GP3 race!** This was in **Barcelona,** on the same weekend as the Spanish Grand Prix.

He won again in **Austria** and **Belgium.** This was good because the track in Austria is quite short while the Belgian circuit at Spa-Francorchamps is one of the longest. Charles was showing his **versatility** by being good on all sorts of race tracks. He was proving to be an all-rounder.

In total, Charles finished on the podium eight times in 2016 and became **GP3 Champion.** Brilliant! Now for Formula 2...

SPRINT FINISH

Charles was signed by **Prema Racing,** the top Italian team who had won the Formula 2 championship in 2016.

There was much more to learn in F2. The cars were more complicated (but not as much as an F1 car!) and the races would be longer than in GP3. Charles learned very quickly.

Like GP3, there would be two Formula 2 races each weekend. There would be a Feature Race with at least one pit stop. On the morning of the following day – the day of the Formula 1 Grand Prix – there would then be a **shorter Sprint Race.**

Pit stops were not necessary in Sprint Races. With the shorter race, a pit stop would lose too much time.

25

But Leclerc and the Prema team had other ideas for the first Sprint Race of the season in Bahrain.

Starting from sixth on the grid, Charles **charged into the lead.** Halfway through the **23-lap** race, he was pulling away from the car in second place.

Then he stopped for fresh tyres. This was a huge surprise! It would cost valuable time coming into the pits and having his mechanics change all four wheels.

Sure enough, Leclerc re-joined in 14th place. He was miles behind the leader. What HAD the Prema team been thinking of? This seemed crazy.

Before the race, Charles and the team had worked out that the car would be slower if he stayed on the same tyres for twenty-three laps. The gamble was that the extra **grip** and **speed** from new tyres would be much better towards the end of the race and allow Leclerc to catch up.

But he was now **twenty-six seconds behind** the leader. He had **thirteen cars to overtake** in just nine laps. This surely could not work?

Charles used the advantage of his new tyres to overtake cars on every lap. With one lap to go, he was third!

Then he was second. Not far from the chequered flag, he snatched the lead and **won the race.** Incredible!

What a way to start his F2 season! The Formula 1 people watching the race were very impressed. Ferrari was delighted that the pupil from their academy had done so well.

F2 CHAMPION

Charles won again at the Feature Race in Spain.

The race he wanted to win most – his home race at **Monaco** - was next.

He started from pole position for the Feature Race and was leading when his car's **suspension** broke. This was very frustrating. Charles had done nothing wrong.

A car's suspension helps to absorb and dampen shock, and helps keep the tyres down on the road. Needless to say, it's very important!

This meant he had to start the Sprint Race from the **back of the grid.** Monaco is a

very narrow circuit. Overtaking is difficult. Leclerc collided with another driver while trying to speed past him.

He was very disappointed. His family home was a few streets away from the race track. Many of his friends from Monaco had been watching this race.

Charles had wanted to do well because Monaco was the race in which his dad had scored his best result by finishing eighth in the Formula 3 race in 1988. That had been a proud moment for Herve Leclerc because the best F3 drivers from around the world had come to race at Monaco.

Charles was also sad for another reason. He had started the F2 season knowing that his father had become ill with cancer. Herve's condition had worsened on the weekend of the Monaco race. The next F2 race was due a month later in Baku, the capital of Azerbaijan.

BAKU: A VERY SAD WIN

Herve Leclerc passed away four days before the Azerbaijan Grand Prix. Charles and his family were devastated.

But they all knew that Herve wanted Charles to continue chasing his dream. Even so, the weekend in Baku would be very tough on nineteen-year-old Charles.

'I tried to focus on the weekend, to get a good result for my father,' said Charles. 'I knew that he wanted me to do one thing: to win.'

The first thing he needed to do was win pole position for the first race, which was the Feature Race.

'It was really difficult,' said Charles. 'I was thinking about my father. I gave it everything.

32

When they came on the radio and told me I had won pole, I was crying. I could not believe it.' Now he needed to follow that very emotional moment with a strong race.

Several drivers crashed into the walls on this difficult track. But Charles put on a brilliant display as he led all the way and **set the fastest lap.**

Icheri Sherer

Khazar

Absheron

Bulvar

Sahil

Maiden Tower

Mugham

Old City

Giz Galasi

ilarmoniya

AzNeft

The rear wing of Charles's race car in Baku carried the message 'JE T'AIME PAPA' ('I LOVE YOU DAD').

He stood on the winner's podium and dedicated the victory to his father.

'I'm here today because of my father,' said Charles. 'He did many things in my career. He has been a huge support for me. This is a good way to thank him.'

YOUNGEST
F2 CHAMPION

Charles continued to race in honour of his dad. He took his **fifth pole position in a row** in Austria and went on to win the Feature Race there, and at **Silverstone** in the supporting race for the British Grand Prix.

In Belgium, on the fast and difficult **Spa-Francorchamps** track, Leclerc started from pole position and won by **twenty seconds.** That's a **huge amount** in such competitive racing.

Unfortunately, his victory was taken from him when part of his car did not meet the regulations. It was not Charles's fault. But he carried on winning with pole position and victory at Jerez in Spain. There was no stopping him!

That gave Charles the **F2 championship with**

three races to go! But he won the last race in Abu Dhabi anyway!

Herve Leclerc would have been very proud. At only nineteen, his son had become the **youngest F2 Champion.** And he had done it in his first season in this super-competitive championship filled with wannabe F1 drivers! More than that, he set a record for winning by the biggest margin – with 282 points, he was seventy-two points ahead of the next closest competitor.

Only **Lewis Hamilton, Nico Rosberg** and **Nico Hülkenberg** had done this in their rookie F2 season. All three had gone on to Formula 1.

The future was looking very bright for Charles.

TEST DRIVING

Being a member of the Ferrari Driver Academy presented great opportunities for Leclerc.

In 2016, Ferrari arranged for Charles to drive a two-year-old F1 car at the team's test track at **Fiorano,** which is next door to the factory. Leclerc completed **186 miles (300 km)** in tricky conditions.

F1 teams are allowed to run rookie drivers during the practice session on the morning of the first day at a Grand Prix. This gives the young driver valuable experience when driving an F1 car and learning about the pressure of being part of a busy Grand Prix weekend.

The 1.9-mile (3 km) track was wet when he started out and drove an F1 car for the first time. He handled this powerful car extremely well on the slippery surface. The team were very impressed. For Charles, it was **a dream come true.**

In 2016, Ferrari arranged for Charles to drive a **Haas–Ferrari** during first practice in the British Grand Prix. He completed twenty-six laps of the Silverstone circuit, made no mistakes and recorded a lap time that was 18th fastest of the twenty-two cars running.

Ferrari supplied Formula 1 engines to Haas and had a good relationship with the Grand Prix team owned by the American, Gene Haas.

Then he did the same thing in Hungary a few weeks later. This time Charles was 15th fastest in the Friday morning practice session at the **Hungaroring.**

Leclerc was offered the opportunity to repeat the experience in Germany and Malaysia, but politely said no. Charles wanted to focus on his GP3 racing which was taking place on the same weekends.

It was a brave decision to turn down the chance of more time in an F1 car. But it was also a sensible choice; Charles **won the GP3 championship!**

JOINING SAUBER

Testing between the Grands Prix is limited to save costs. During the 2017 F1 season, there was one test session. This was at the Hungaroring in July.

McLaren used this test session to give **Lando Norris** his first experience in an F1 car. Mercedes did the same with **George Russell.** And Ferrari used the opportunity to give **Charles Leclerc** some serious running in their latest F1 car.

Charles completed **ninety-eight laps.** He was the **fastest of all the twelve drivers** running that day. His lap time was just 1.5 seconds slower than the pole position time set for the Hungarian Grand Prix which had been held a few days before.

It would have put Charles ninth on the grid for the Grand Prix. Amazing!

'I love the car!' said Charles. 'It's quite a big step – but I feel ready. I don't think there are any more steps I need to do before coming to Formula 1.'

Ferrari was convinced. An arrangement was made to loan Charles to **Sauber** for 2018.

Like Haas, Sauber also used Ferrari engines. The small team from **Switzerland** was an ideal place for a young driver to start in Formula 1. There would be less pressure on a novice there than if he had started with a bigger team like Ferrari, Mercedes or Red Bull.

Sauber was well known for helping develop drivers who would go on to race for Ferrari.

Jean Alesi from France and **Felipe Massa** from Brazil had raced for Sauber before winning races for Ferrari.

In 2001, Sauber had taken a very big gamble by giving a drive to **Kimi Räikkönen.** The young Finnish driver had very little experience. But he went on to join Ferrari and become **World Champion in 2007.**

KIMI RÄIKKÖNEN

Kimi Räikkönen was known as '**The Iceman**'.
He was very quiet and **very cool.** He had
'ICEMAN' painted on his blue and white crash
helmet.

Blue and white are the colours of **Finland,** where Räikkönen was born in 1979.

He is the most successful Finnish racing driver of all time. He won twenty-one Formula 1 races and started 349 Grands Prix when racing for Sauber, McLaren, Ferrari, Lotus and Alfa Romeo.

Räikkönen started racing karts when he was ten. He later moved up to racing single-seater cars and won a championship in Scandinavia. Scandinavia is made up of Norway, Sweden and Denmark, countries that are close to Finland.

Sauber gave Räikkönen a test in their Formula 1 car. He was so fast, **Peter Sauber,** the man who owned the team, decided to give Kimi a Grand Prix drive.

This was a HUGE gamble. Räikkönen had competed in only twenty-three car races – EVER. People said he would not be ready for the pressure and speed of Formula 1. They said this was a crazy decision!

Kimi didn't care what people said. He would prove his critics wrong and Mr Sauber right.

This was one of the most exciting moments of his life. And yet Kimi was so cool and relaxed that he was taking a nap just thirty minutes before making his F1 debut in the 2001 Australian Grand Prix! Then he went and scored a championship point in the race. Amazing!

Räikkönen was signed by McLaren and scored a podium in his first race for the famous British team.

He won for the first time in Malaysia in 2003 and finished second in the World Championship.

After five years with McLaren, Kimi moved to Ferrari in 2007, won six races and became **World Champion.** Now he was REALLY cool!

MARCUS ERICSSON

Marcus Ericsson is a Swedish racing driver. He was Charles Leclerc's **teammate** in 2018 when Charles made his F1 debut with Sauber.

They raced together for one season. Leclerc scored thirty more points than Ericsson. Charles said he learned a lot from Marcus.

In 2019, Ericsson switched from Formula 1 to **IndyCar racing** in North America. He **won the famous Indianapolis 500 in 2022.** This is also known as the 'Indy 500'. It is held on a huge oval track. The cars go left all the time. There are no right-hand corners! This was a fantastic result which made Ericsson very well known in the USA.

Ericsson painted his crash helmet in the blue and yellow colours of Ronnie Peterson to honour the legendary Swedish F1 driver.

Peterson had been runner-up twice in the F1 World Championship. He died following a crash during the 1978 Italian Grand Prix. Peterson had been a hero of Ericsson when Marcus was growing up. Stories like his show just how high the stakes are in Formula One. The dangers of racing go far beyond just losing.

INTO FORMULA 1

Charles Leclerc chose number **16** when he began F1 with Sauber in 2018. Seven is his favourite number, but it was already allocated to Kimi Räikkönen! So Charles went for 16 because it is the date of his birth (16 October) and because 1+6 = 7.

If you were racing, what would your number be?

His first F1 Grand Prix was in Australia. Charles had never raced in **Melbourne** before. He took time to get used to the car and the track and managed to qualify just one tenth of a second behind Marcus Ericsson who had raced on the Albert Park circuit four times before.

One tenth of a second – that's quicker than the click of a finger! That's how fine the margins in Formula 1 racing are.

Leclerc made no mistakes. He brought his Sauber home in **13th place** and on the same lap as **Sebastian Vettel** in the winning Ferrari. (Ericsson had retired early in the race with a

technical problem). It was an encouraging start for Leclerc.

Charles **spun** the Sauber a few times during practice at the next races in **Bahrain** and **China**. There was a worry that if he did spin his car at the fourth race in **Azerbaijan,** it could be serious because the street circuit was lined by concrete walls. There would be no room at all for errors.

But Charles loved the **Baku** circuit. It was where he had scored that very important win in F2 the year before.

Charles had also been working hard, learning about the Sauber car and how it required a different driving technique from the F2 and GP3 cars he had been used to over the past few years. The secret was not to be so aggressive with the Sauber. And it worked!

He qualified 14th (four places ahead of Ericsson) and drove a brilliant race. Charles overtook one of his heroes, **Fernando Alonso,** on his way

to sixth place. That meant eight championship points. Fantastic!

The Sauber team was delighted. It was their best result in three years!

Now Charles was really looking forward to racing a Formula 1 car for the first time in the **Monaco Grand Prix.**

For his home race, Charles had his crash helmet painted in the design used by his father, Herve, when he raced in F3 at Monaco. This would be a very special occasion for the Leclerc family.

Charles qualified 14th – ahead of both Haas-Ferraris and the Sauber of his teammate, Marcus Ericsson.

In the race he was driving beautifully. Then, just eight laps from the finish, a **front brake failed** and caused the Sauber to **crash** into the back of another car!

51

Neither driver was hurt but Leclerc was very disappointed to have to retire after having done so well and seriously challenging for 11th place.

Once again, his homecoming race had been decided by matters outside of his control.

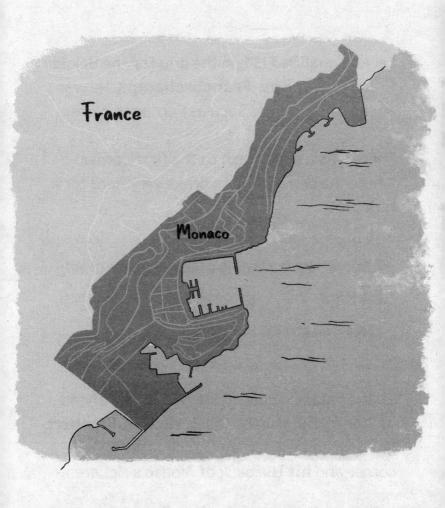

A LUCKY ESCAPE

Leclerc qualified 13th on the grid for the Belgian Grand Prix at **Spa-Francorchamps.** He was ahead of big names such as Fernando Alonso.

There was a short dash to the first corner, where the drivers had to brake very hard for a **hairpin.**

> A hairpin turn is a bend in a road where the driver has to turn 180°. They can be very tricky at normal speeds, let alone in an F1 car!

Charles made a good start and stayed ahead of Alonso. But, further back, **Nico Hülkenberg** got it wrong when they reached the first corner and **hit** the back of Alonso's McLaren.

This **pushed** Alonso into Leclerc. The McLaren went into the air and **landed on top** of Leclerc's Sauber before **bouncing** off.

Charles was saved by the **halo,** a very strong hoop above his head. The halo had big black marks caused by a tyre from Alonso's car.

Had the halo not been there, the McLaren would have landed directly on Charles's head.

Leclerc's Sauber was badly damaged by the accident. He could not continue with the race in Belgium. But he could hardly wait to go racing again.

'Accidents happen in motor racing,' said Charles. 'I have absolutely no fear in a racing car.'

Leclerc qualified in an amazing seventh place for the race in Russia. And he finished in the same position – his best result so far in F1. Not many people expected this.

As if to prove how promising he was, Charles

finished seventh **three more times** – in Mexico, Brazil and Abu Dhabi.

At the end of his first season of F1 Charles Leclerc was **13th in the World Championship.**

It was a brilliant debut by the **twenty-one-year-old** from Monaco. Ferrari was so impressed that they decided to make Charles part of their F1 team for 2019. He would be teammate to **Sebastian Vettel,** the four-time World Champion. Praise didn't come higher than that.

'Autosprint', a leading motor sport magazine in Italy, gave Leclerc their prestigious 'Golden Helmet' award.

He was voted '**F1 Rookie of the Year**' by the FIA, motor sport's governing body, and by 'Autosport' magazine in the UK.

'Autocourse' the highly respected Formula 1 annual, rated Leclerc No. 7 in their esteemed 'Driver Top 10'.

LOUIS CHIRON

When Charles Leclerc finished sixth in the Azerbaijan Grand Prix, he became the first driver from Monaco to have scored world championship points since **Louis Chiron** – way back in 1950!

When Louis was little, he was a bellboy in Monaco's famous and very grand **Hotel de Paris.**

He fell in love with cars thanks to the very fancy motorcars driven by guests when they arrived at the hotel.

A rich friend lent Louis a car to go racing. He was very successful.

When given a drive by **Bugatti** – a really famous team using their Bugatti cars built in France – Chiron won many Grands Prix, including the Monaco Grand Prix in 1931.

Chiron also raced for **Enzo Ferrari** – another connection between the man from Monaco and Charles Leclerc.

Before he retired from racing, Louis Chiron became the oldest man to have started a Formula 1 Grand Prix. When Chiron finished sixth in the 1955 Monaco Grand Prix, he was **fifty-five!**

Louis Chiron helped organize the Monaco Grand Prix. There is a statue in Chiron's honour, a few minutes' walk from where Charles Leclerc grew up!

SCUDERIA FERRARI

The Ferrari team has been in Formula 1 longer than anyone else.

The famous Italian team has **raced in every F1 World Championship** since the competition started in 1950.

Ferrari has competed in **over 1,000 Grands Prix** and won more than **240 F1 races.** That's a huge number!

1947 166 Spyder Corsa

Many famous names in motor racing – **Alberto Ascari, Juan Manuel Fangio, Michael Schumacher** – are among the drivers to have **won 15 World Championships** for Ferrari.

The team, called Scuderia Ferrari, was started by Enzo Ferrari.

The first Ferrari was raced in **1930.** This was a sports car.

Then Ferrari built a Grand Prix car – and that's when the legend really began.

Ferraris were always red. Enzo Ferrari adopted the symbol of a black prancing horse on a yellow shield. This badge has been on every Ferrari ever made.

Enzo built his own engines. Some were small with four cylinders. The largest had **twelve cylinders** and made a fantastic sound!

Mike Hawthorn drove for Ferrari in 1958, the year he became the very first F1 World Champion from Great Britain.

Another Englishman, **John Surtees,** won the World Championship with Ferrari in 1964.

Drivers see it as an **exciting honour** to race for Ferrari. It was a dream of Charles Leclerc's. He was thrilled to become a Ferrari F1 driver in 2019.

Even Lewis Hamilton has been tempted to leave Mercedes and join Ferrari in 2025!

Nigel Mansell was another great British F1 champion to drive the red cars.

In the Saudi Arabian Grand Prix in 2024, Oliver Bearman made his F1 debut with Ferrari and drove brilliantly to finish seventh and score points in his first Grand Prix.

Oliver was just eighteen years old. He comes from Chelmsford in Essex and became the youngest British driver to become part of the Ferrari legend.

HISTORY OF FERRARI

Ferrari is one of the most famous names in the world of motoring. The Italian company makes beautiful cars that are **fast** – and **expensive!**

You can pay anything from £275,000 to £730,000 for one of these exotic sports cars.

What would your dream car be if you had an unlimited amount of money?

Enzo Ferrari made his first road car in **1947.** This was a two-seater sports car known as the **Ferrari 125 S.** Only two were built.

One of his most famous cars was the **Ferrari 250 GTO.** Thirty-six of these beautiful sports cars were made between 1962 and 1964.

 62

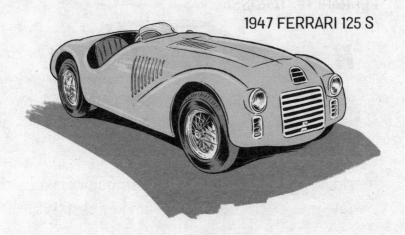

1947 FERRARI 125 S

The Ferrari 250 GTO went on sale in the United States of America for $18,000 (£14,000). That was a lot of money in 1962!

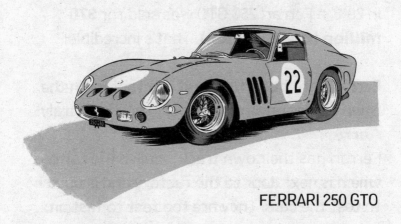

FERRARI 250 GTO

63

FERRARI TESTAROSSA

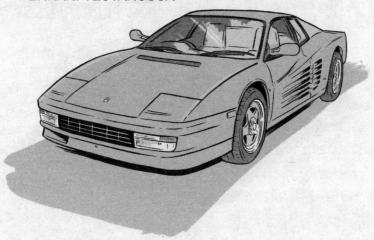

The Ferrari 250 GTO has become one of the most desirable cars in the world. Very few are remaining.

In 2018, a Ferrari 250 GTO was sold for **$70 million (£54.6 million).** That's incredible!

Ferraris are **built by hand** in a factory in the town of **Maranello,** which is in northern Italy.

Ferrari has their own track – called **Fiorano** – which is next door to the factory and is used to test the cars. They are too fast to test on normal roads!

The **Ferrari SF90 XX** is the most powerful Ferrari road car ever made. It can exceed **150 mph (241 kmh)!** This car went on sale in 2024.

Ferrari will make 799 of the **SF90 XX Stradale** with a hard top, and 599 of the **Spyder,** which has an open top. Every single one has been sold! That's nearly £1,000 million in total!

FERRARI ENZO

The legend of this great name continues more than seventy years after the first Ferrari appeared.

ENZO FERRARI

Enzo Ferrari was a racing driver when he was young. He **won three Grands Prix** in 1923 when he was twenty-five years old.

Then Enzo decided he was better at running a team than being a racing driver.

The Scuderia Ferrari team was started in **1929** when Enzo Ferrari entered cars in races for **Alfa Romeo,** the famous Italian car marker.

Once Ferrari had begun to build his own cars, he became famous in the world of motor racing as his cars won races. Ferrari started with sports cars and then built cars for Formula 1. Ferrari also built cars for the road. He used the money made from these beautiful cars to pay for his racing team and building Formula 1 cars.

Enzo Ferrari was a tough boss. But drivers liked to race for him because he built fast cars. He became a **legend.**

I interviewed Enzo Ferrari once in his office at the headquarters in Modena in Italy. There was not much light in the room and he wore dark glasses. He spoke very quietly in Italian. His assistant translated for me. It was a spooky experience! But unforgettable. I was talking with a **Racing Legend!**

LECLERC'S FIRST FERRARI GRAND PRIX

There was a lot of excitement in Formula 1 at the start of the 2019 season. How would Charles Leclerc get on with his Ferrari teammate, Sebastian Vettel?

Would Charles be as fast as the **four-time World Champion?** Would he be FASTER? Some F1 experts thought that might be possible. Leclerc was that good!

As far as Charles was concerned, he couldn't wait to put on the **red Ferrari overalls** with the famous yellow badge and the black prancing horse.

Being a Ferrari driver was a massive honour. But it might also bring pressure for such a young driver.

How was Charles going to get on at the first Grand Prix in Australia?

Ferrari was rather shocked at the speed of the Mercedes cars as **Valtteri Bottas** and **Lewis Hamilton** set the fastest times in qualifying. Sebastian was third fastest. Charles was fifth fastest.

Valtteri Bottas is a driver from Finland, like Kimi Räikkönen.

Charles had made a **small mistake** on his best lap. This may have been his best-ever qualifying in F1 – but he was disappointed!

The expectations were much higher now that he was with Ferrari and not Sauber. That's what happens when you step up to a big team that's used to winning.

Mercedes finished the race first and second, with Bottas in front of Hamilton, the reigning

World Champion. Max Verstappen's Red Bull was third.

Sebastian was a close fourth with Charles right behind his teammate in fifth place. He could have done no more.

It was a very good start to Charles's career with such a great team.

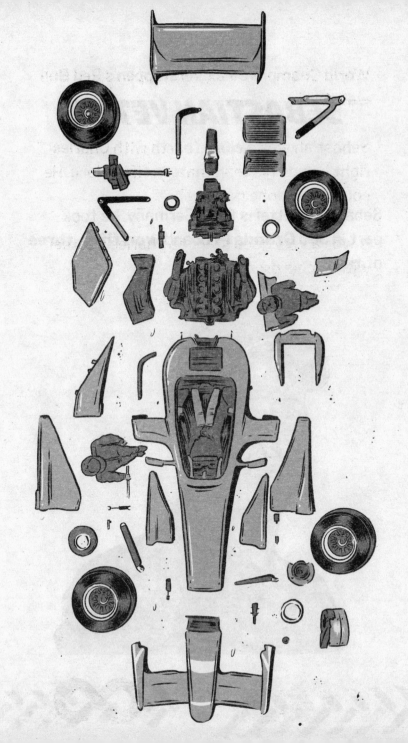

SEBASTIAN VETTEL

Sebastian Vettel is from Germany. He took part in **300 Grands Prix** and **won fifty-three** of them.

Vettel is one of the **most successful F1 drivers ever.**

He won **four World Championships.**

Only **Lewis Hamilton, Michael Schumacher** and **Juan Manuel Fangio** have won more than four.

Sebastian first drove a kart when he was just three years old! He was racing karts five years later – and winning races.

Vettel's hero was Michael Schumacher. When he saw Schumacher win the 1995 German Grand Prix at Hockenheim – which was near Sebastian's home – he was inspired and more determined than ever to become a Formula 1 driver. Sebastian was eight years old.

The Sauber team gave Vettel his big F1 chance.

When one of the Sauber drivers was injured, Vettel was chosen to take his place in the 2007 United States Grand Prix. Vettel finished eighth. At the time, he was the **youngest driver to score a championship point.** Sebastian was **nineteen years old.**

In 2008, Red Bull made Vettel part of their F1 junior team known as **Toro Rosso.** He scored a stunning win in the **Italian Grand Prix.**

He led most of the way and did not make any mistakes despite the track being very slippery because of rain. This was VERY impressive for a driver so young and inexperienced.

Red Bull made Vettel part of their core team. He scored **Red Bull's very first Grand Prix win** in China in 2009.

That was the start of incredible success for Vettel and Red Bull.

They won the championship **four years running,** starting in 2010.

In 2015, he moved to Ferrari and won races. This was very emotional for Sebastian as his hero, Michael Schumacher, had won many races and championships with Ferrari.

For his final years in Formula 1, Sebastian raced with Aston Martin until he **retired at the end of 2022.**

SO CLOSE TO
A FIRST WIN

At the start of the 2019 season, Formula 1 moved from the city of Melbourne to the desert of Bahrain.

The **Sakhir track** in Bahrain would be very different from **Albert Park** in Australia. But the Ferrari felt good here. And Charles loved the track.

He loved it so much, he **won his first pole position in Formula 1!** He was faster than Sebastian Vettel in the other Ferrari and ahead of the Mercedes team – who were the World Champions.

It was a brilliant performance by Charles as he became the second youngest driver ever in F1 to win a pole position.

The actual race was held under floodlights on a warm evening.

Charles did not make a good start and found himself falling back to third place behind Valtteri Bottas and Vettel.

On the second lap, Charles took second place from the Mercedes of Bottas and chased after Vettel.

On the sixth lap, Charles passed his teammate and **led a Grand Prix** for the first time!
It was **only his second race** for Ferrari.
Unbelievable!

Vettel could not catch Leclerc. This was looking good! Could Charles really win his first Grand Prix so soon?

It looked like he could.

Then – **disaster!**

With ten laps to go, Charles felt something go

wrong with his **engine.** The Ferrari started to slow down. There was nothing he could do!

Lewis Hamilton overtook the Ferrari. And then the Mercedes of Bottas overtook Charles.

Leclerc hung on to third place. He **finished on the podium** for the first time. But he could have won.

Charles was disappointed. But he didn't show it.

'It's part of motor racing,' said Charles. 'Unfortunately it was not our day.'

Lewis came over to Charles and consoled him. Lewis had been in the same situation when he was younger. He understood exactly how Charles was feeling.

When interviewed by the press and asked about Leclerc, Hamilton said: 'He did a fantastic weekend. He has a bright future ahead of him.'

Praise did not come much higher than that.

BAHRAIN GRAND PRIX

Bahrain was the first country in the Middle East to hold a Formula 1 Grand Prix. This was in 2004.

The first race was won by the Ferrari of Michael Schumacher. The German driver would win his **seventh World Championship** that year, a record that has been matched by Lewis Hamilton.

The Bahrain circuit is in **Sakhir,** an area which is 20 miles (32 km) from the country's capital, **Manama.**

Sakhir is in the desert and was built on the site of what had once been a farm for camels!

 79

Because of the warm weather in January and February, the Bahrain track has been used for testing when the F1 teams run their cars for the first time before the season starts.

Bahrain has staged the first race of the season several times.

In 2014, the Grand Prix was held at night for the first time. This meant the race was not so tough on the drivers because it was not so hot and there was less humidity.

When F1 was looking for countries to stage Grands Prix during the Covid-19 pandemic in 2020, Bahrain came to the rescue by running two races one week after the other.

To give the drivers a different challenge, the owners of Sakhir adapted the circuit for the

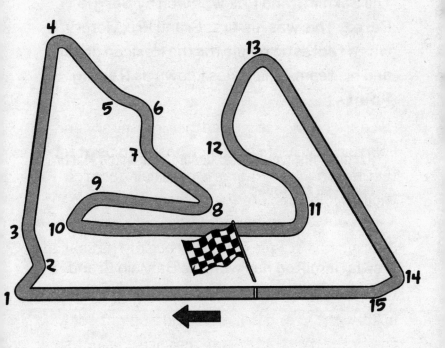

second race by cutting out the middle section of the track.

This race was known as the Sakhir Grand Prix. It took just **fifty-three seconds** to complete a lap around the outer loop! (The main circuit took drivers almost a minute and a half to complete a lap.)

The Sakhir Grand Prix was won by **Sergio Perez.** This was his first Grand Prix victory. It was a fantastic result for the Mexican driver and his team, which was known as **Racing Point.**

Racing Point would later become the Aston Martin team you see today.

Lewis Hamilton has won the Bahrain Grand Prix **five times.**

GILLES VILLENEUVE

Gilles Villeneuve raced for Ferrari and won
six Grands Prix. He was a spectacular driver
who **loved going fast.**

Gilles was born in **Canada** in 1950. From an early age, he raced **snowmobiles** in Quebec, which is a province of Canada. It snows a lot during the winter in Quebec.

As soon as he was old enough, Villeneuve raced cars and won championships in Canada and across the border in the United States of America.

Gilles was so good that the **McLaren** F1 team gave him a drive in the 1977 British Grand Prix at Silverstone. He finished 11th after a delay in the pits. But he had done enough to earn a place on the Ferrari team in 1978.

Villeneuve won his first Grand Prix in **September 1978.** It was an emotional day. This was in his home race in Canada, and the first time a new circuit in Montreal had been used.

Very sadly, Gilles was killed in a collision during qualifying for the 1982 Belgian Grand Prix at **Zolder.** The track in Montreal was named

 84

'Circuit Gilles Villeneuve' in his honour.

Jacques – Gilles' son – would continue the Villeneuve legend by becoming a racing driver and **winning the 1997 F1 World Championship** with the Williams team.

CHARLES'S FIRST FERRARI SEASON

The first half of the 2019 season was very difficult for Leclerc. The Ferrari car had promise – but **things kept going wrong.**

Charles finished fifth in China, Azerbaijan and Spain. He had hoped for better results – particularly after nearly winning in Bahrain. Monaco was next!

The Ferrari was expected to be quick on Leclerc's home track. This was looking good – particularly when Charles was fastest during final practice on Saturday morning.

If he could qualify on pole position in the afternoon, that would be brilliant. Because Monaco is such a tight and narrow circuit, the driver who starts from pole position has a **big advantage.** Other drivers find it hard to overtake!

Qualifying is in three parts, called Q1, Q2 and Q3.

All twenty drivers take part in Q1. The **fastest fifteen drivers** then move onto Q2. When Q2 is finished, only the **fastest ten drivers** make it to Q3.

That's when qualifying becomes really tense! The fastest driver in Q3 will take the coveted **pole position!**

Charles had done it once before in Bahrain. Could he do it in Monaco? He was sure that he could.

He set a time early in Q1. The Ferrari team thought that would be fast enough to get Leclerc into Q2. But they made a mistake! Charles's time was NOT good enough. He was only **16th** fastest and would not go forward with the fastest fifteen to Q2. What a **disaster!** Charles was devastated. The Monaco Grand Prix would be really hard because he was starting near the back of the field.

Charles did the best he could. He fought his way into **12th place** but a misunderstanding as he tried to overtake another car meant the Ferrari hit the wall. This **punctured a tyre.**

By the time Leclerc struggled back to the pits, he was **last.** The damage meant there was no point in continuing.

This was massively disappointing for everyone, including the many Leclerc fans waving Ferrari flags in the grandstands.

But everyone believed that a win for Charles was not far away. The first half of the 2019 season had its disappointments but, overall, Charles had done well.

He had finished on the podium **five times** – including a brilliant second place in Austria. It would not be long before Leclerc stood on the top step of the podium.

WINNING FOR HIS FRIEND, ANTHOINE

Anthoine Hubert was a young racing driver from France. Charles had raced against Anthoine in karts when they were little. They became very good friends.

Hubert had **followed the same path** as Leclerc by racing in Formula Renault and GP3.

When Charles became a Ferrari driver in 2019, he was very happy to see Anthoine race in Formula 2. The Formula 2 races would be taking place on Grand Prix weekends. Charles was able to keep an eye on his friend's progress.

By the time they reached the Belgian Grand Prix at the end of August, Hubert had won two Formula 2 races. He was showing great promise.

Then, in the Formula 2 race, one driver crashed on a very fast corner and triggered a **collision with four cars.** Anthoine Hubert's car was one of them. He was badly injured. Sadly, the track's doctors could not save him.

Safety has improved so much in motor racing but accidents sometimes happen. Charles was devastated over the loss of his friend.

Charles won pole position that afternoon. He said he would race in the next day's Grand Prix in honour of Anthoine.

Leclerc took the lead at the first corner and stayed in front all the way. He came under **huge pressure** from Lewis Hamilton in the final laps.

But nothing was going to stop Charles from **winning his first Grand Prix** – and doing it in a Ferrari!

It was a fantastic result. But no one felt like celebrating. There was no champagne on the

podium. Charles received the winner's trophy –
and then looked up to the sky, remembering his
dear friend, Anthoine. It was bittersweet.

'I can't enjoy fully my first victory,' said
Charles. 'But it will definitely be a memory I will
keep forever – for some sad reasons and for
some good reasons.'

MADNESS AT MONZA

The Italian Grand Prix was next. This is held at **Monza**, one of the **oldest motor racing circuits** in the world.

Monza is very fast. It is also the home circuit of Ferrari. The Ferrari fans are so passionate! The atmosphere is ELECTRIC!

Following Leclerc's win in Belgium, Monza was even madder than usual!

More than **100,000 fans** – most of them Ferrari supporters – came to Monza hoping for another victory.

Leclerc was mobbed wherever he went. He had become the new **Ferrari hero.**

Now he had to do the business on the race

track. The Tifosi expected nothing less!

Ferrari fans are known as the 'Tifosi'. This comes from the word 'typhos', which means smoke. This is because, in Ancient Greece, fans used to gather around bonfires after seeing their favourite athletes perform.

Charles was **fastest in qualifying.** It meant a Ferrari was on pole at Monza. It was a great start – but this meant the **pressure on him was even greater!**

Charles took the lead at the start. For **fifty-three laps** of this super-fast track, he came under huge pressure from **Lewis Hamilton** in his Mercedes.

But Charles didn't crack! He remained **incredibly cool** and was first to reach the chequered flag.

It was his second win in a week! But this one

would be very different. It was at Monza and he could really **celebrate** this time after the sadness in Belgium.

The podium at Monza is amazing. It stretches to the edge of the track. The Tifosi **climbed the fences** and **crowded onto the track** beneath the podium. They were waving red Ferrari flags and banners with '16' – the number on Leclerc's Ferrari.

There was loud cheering and red smoke as Charles looked down on hundreds of very happy faces, chanting his name.

SHIFTING GEARS

Leclerc was starting in pole position for the next race in **Singapore**. Many in F1 said this was the **most brilliant lap of the season.** The circuit is on the streets of the city. The track is **bumpy, fast** and **demanding.**

Charles finished second this time, behind his Ferrari teammate Sebastian Vettel.

Charles would finish on the podium **two more times** in 2019 and win **two more pole positions.**

He **finished fourth in the World Championship.** It had been a very impressive first season with Ferrari.

'Autocourse' placed Leclerc No. 3 in their Top 10 driver rating. 'Leclerc's win at Monza was the

95

stuff of dreams,' wrote the annual's editor.

Lewis Hamilton (the World Champion) was
voted No. 1 by 'Autocourse'. Lewis had won
eleven times in 2019. Max Verstappen was voted
No. 2 after winning three Grands Prix.

Leclerc and Verstappen were about to become
great rivals in F1. This was nothing new! They
had fought many battles when racing karts.

RACE MAXIMUM SPEEDS	
SPEED TRAP	KM/H
C LECLERC	207.4
M VERSTAPPEN	207.1
L HAMILTON	206.8
L NORRIS	206.7

RIVALRY WITH MAX VERSTAPPEN

Charles Leclerc and Max Verstappen raced against each other many times when karting.

Sometimes their battles became serious. In one kart race in 2012, they **collided.** Each driver blamed the other!

'Sometimes, our races didn't end in the best way!' says Charles. 'When we were about twelve years old, Max was leading one race and our karts touched as I overtook. At the next corner – he destroyed me! I lost a lot of places!'

Max explains his side of the story. 'I'm leading. He wants to pass and he pushes me, and I push him back, and after, he pushes me off the track!'

The race officials **disqualified** BOTH drivers! It was a strong lesson for Max and Charles.

Motor racing can be a dangerous sport. It's silly to take too many risks.

Max and Charles had learned a lot since then. They had **great respect** for each other when they began racing in Grands Prix.

When Leclerc made his F1 debut in 2018, Verstappen was with Red Bull and had already won **three Grands Prix.**

They would begin to race wheel-to-wheel again when Charles moved up to

Ferrari in 2019. The old friends were continuing where they had left off when karting eight years before!

Verstappen reached F1 first. He had his first F1 race in 2015. When Max raced in Australia in 2015, he became the youngest driver to take part in a Grand Prix.

LECLERC

Born	16.10.97
First Grand Prix	2018 Australia
First World Championship points	2018 Azerbaijan
First F1 podium	2019 Bahrain
First Pole Position	2019 Austria
Pole Positions	23*
First Fastest Lap	2019 Bahrain
Fastest Laps	9*
Laps in the lead	660+
First F1 win	2019 Belgium
Most F1 wins in a season	3 (2022)
F1 wins	5*
F1 Podiums	32*
F1 World Championships	0
Championship points	1121*
Grands Prix raced	126*

* As of March 2024

Vs VERSTAPPEN

30.9.97

2015 Australia

2015 Malaysia

2016 Spain

2019 Hungary

35*

2016 Brazil

31*

2900+

2016 Spain

19 (2023)

56*

100*

3

2640*

188*

POLE POSITION

Each lap time of every driver is recorded during Qualifying.

The driver with the **fastest lap** wins Pole Position.

Pole Position is at the very front of the starting grid. That's a **big advantage** compared to the slowest driver during Qualifying. The slowest driver starts from the back of the grid in **20th place.**

Winning Pole Position says you are the Fastest Driver. It is an honour that not many drivers achieve.

Lewis Hamilton has won more Pole Positions than any other driver. He has

102

started from Pole Position an amazing **104 times!**

Michael Schumacher comes next. The seven-time World Champion won **68 Pole Positions.**

The legendary **Ayrton Senna** is not far behind with **65 Pole Positions.**

Of the twenty drivers racing in Formula 1 in 2024, more than half have won a Pole Position.

Max Verstappen has won the most with more than **35.**

Charles Leclerc comes next with **23.**

Then it's **Fernando Alonso** (22) and **Valtteri Bottas** (20).

Leclerc's teammate, **Carlos Sainz,** has won 5.

More than 100 drivers have won Pole Position in the seventy-four-year history of Formula 1 Grand Prix racing.

The youngest was Sebastian Vettel. He was twenty-one years old when he won Pole Position for the 2008 Italian Grand Prix.

The oldest was Giuseppe Farina. The 1950 World Champion was forty-seven when he won Pole Position in the Argentine Grand Prix in 1954!

You might think that a driver starting from Pole Position will always win the race. They are starting ahead of everyone else!

But this does not happen as often as you might think.

Grand Prix racing is so close and so competitive that another driver could overtake the Pole Position driver during the charge to the first corner!

 104

A Grand Prix is long. It usually runs for at least an **hour and a half.** During that time, each driver must make at least one pit stop.

This is an ideal chance for another driver to overtake the leader.

The driver on Pole Position needs to **concentrate** very hard all the way to the finish.

But they also need to look after their tyres and their car. And not make any mistakes!

Lewis Hamilton has won the most races after starting from Pole Position. That's no surprise because Lewis has started from Pole Position more often than anyone else. He has **won more than sixty races from Pole Position.**

Max Verstappen is next with at least thirty wins from Pole Position.

Charles Leclerc has **won four of the five races** he started from Pole Position.

 105

A LEGEND AMONG LEGENDS

 Jenson Button

(2009 F1 World Champion)

'Charles Leclerc is every bit as quick as everyone else, if not the fastest driver in terms of raw pace.'

 Carlos Sainz

(Winner 2024 Australian Grand Prix)

'He's driving at a very high level. He's putting together super-impressive lap times.'

 Fernando Alonso

(2005, 2006 World Champion)

'He is young, intelligent and talented.'

Sebastian Vettel

(2010, 2011, 2012, 2013 World Champion)

'Charles beat me fairly (when we raced together at Ferrari). He was very fast. I think he will go a long way if he has the right equipment. We saw it immediately when he came into F1.'

Max Verstappen

(2021, 2022, 2023 World Champion)

'I think Charles is one of the most talented drivers in Formula 1. He will win many more races. We are just good competitors and we like racing. You can see that when we are battling hard.'

Sir Lewis Hamilton

(2008, 2014, 2015, 2017, 2018, 2019, 2020 World Champion)

'It's great to see how Charles has grown. He's still young and he has the class to grow even further and become even stronger. I've looked forward to racing together.'

NIKI LAUDA

Niki Lauda is one of the **most famous drivers** in the history of F1.

Lauda was born in **Vienna,** the capital of Austria.

He won **twenty-five Grands Prix** and was World Champion three times. He is the only driver yet to have won championships with **Ferrari** and **McLaren,** two of the greatest names in Formula 1.

Lauda won his first World Championship in **1975** when driving for Ferrari.

In 1976 he had a terrible accident when his Ferrari **crashed** and **caught fire** during the German Grand Prix. Lauda was badly burned. He was lucky to survive.

Unbelievably, he was racing again just **six weeks later.** Lauda was in a fantastic fight for the championship in 1976 and lost by one point to Britain's **James Hunt** in a McLaren.

Lauda won his second championship with Ferrari in 1977.

He switched to the **Brabham team** in 1978 and retired from motor racing in 1979.

During his break from motor racing, Niki Lauda started his own airline, Lauda Air.

He was an accomplished pilot. He could fly all of the aircraft in the Lauda Air fleet. That included aeroplanes as big as the Boeing 777!

But he came back to motor racing in **1982.** He joined McLaren – and won a third championship in 1984! Incredible!

He stopped racing for good in 1985 and later became an advisor to the Mercedes team. Lauda was responsible for persuading Lewis Hamilton to leave McLaren and join Mercedes – where Lewis won six World Championships!

2020 SEASON

After an exciting first year with Ferrari, the next season in 2020 was a **big disappointment** for Charles Leclerc.

The Ferrari was not good in 2020. Charles struggled to make the car work. Even his team-mate, Sebastian Vettel, could not do anything with this Ferrari. And Vettel had won four World Championships and fifty-three Grands Prix!

2020 was a difficult year for everyone. This was when the Covid-19 pandemic meant there was very little sport.

But Formula 1 managed to put on seventeen races. Spectators were not allowed into many of the Grands Prix because of Covid. The races

were held in front of empty grandstands. The drivers found it very strange not to have cheering crowds!

Leclerc got off to a good start when he **finished second at the first Grand Prix** in Austria. This was a very good result because Charles had started from a disappointing seventh on the grid.

Problems for other drivers ahead meant Leclerc found himself on the podium when he least expected it.

Good tactics by Ferrari brought third place for Leclerc in the British Grand Prix.

But after that, his results were poor.

A good example was the Belgian Grand Prix, a race Charles had won the year before on a circuit he loves.

He could make the Ferrari go no faster than 13th on the grid. He was nowhere in the race and finished 14th!

Charles finished the season **eighth in the championship,** miles behind Lewis Hamilton who became World Champion for the seventh time.

It was even worse for Vettel, who finished 13th.

But the good thing was that the 'Autocourse' annual placed Leclerc third in the drivers' Top 10 for 2020. His car may have been poor but Charles had not lost his ability or promise. He still looked fast!

2021 *had* to be better!

A NEW TEAMMATE

Charles Leclerc had a new teammate at Ferrari in 2021.

When Sebastian Vettel left Ferrari, he was replaced by **Carlos Sainz** from **Spain.**

Carlos is from a famous motor sport family. His father – who is also called Carlos – was **World Rally Champion** in 1990 and 1992.

Carlos's father helped him get started in motor sport. Like many young racing drivers, Carlos began by racing karts and he won a championship when he was fourteen.

When he moved into racing cars, Sainz won championships in Formula Renault and Formula 3.5.

He was chosen by Red Bull to make his Formula 1 debut with their junior team, **Toro Rosso,** in 2015.

Then he moved to the Renault F1 team in 2017 and, two years later, Sainz raced for McLaren. He finished third in the Brazilian Grand Prix in 2019 before joining Ferrari in 2021.

It was going to be interesting to see who would be the faster driver: Carlos or Charles?

ANOTHER HOMECOMING

Charles couldn't wait for another chance to race in the Monaco Grand Prix.

This was his **home race.** But he'd never had much luck in Monaco.

There had been the mistake by the Ferrari team during qualifying in 2019. The Monaco Grand Prix didn't take place because of Covid-19 in 2020. But now F1 was back on the spectacular street circuit.

Leclerc was the favourite to win. The Ferrari would be fast on the narrow street circuit.

Charles was **quickest** in one of the practice sessions. Could he continue this into qualifying? This would decide grid positions for the Grand Prix.

Charles had painted his crash helmet in the colours of Louis Chiron as a tribute to the man from Monaco who had won this race ninety years before!

Leclerc produced a brilliant lap to go fastest! But he knew others – Max Verstappen in the Red Bull, for instance! – might beat his time in the final minutes of qualifying.

So, Charles went out for one more lap – and tried too hard! He **hit the barrier!** Qualifying was stopped. No one could improve on Leclerc's time. He would start this important race from pole!

The Ferrari **mechanics** repaired the damaged car in time for the race. But they did not realize that the crash had damaged a part inside the **gearbox.** It could not be seen when the mechanics checked the car.

As Charles drove from the pits to the starting grid, he could feel something was wrong.

Then the gearbox broke. NO!!! This was unbelievable.

He would not be able to take part in such an important race.

Charles was massively **disappointed.** So were his many friends in Monaco and the thousands of Ferrari fans in the grandstands.

Would his bad luck at Monaco never end?

 122

BACK TO BAKU

Rather than be angry and upset, Charles quickly put what happened at Monaco behind him – and took pole position at the very next race in **Azerbaijan!**

This was at **Baku.** Like Monaco, Baku is a **street circuit** with the walls and barriers **very close** to the edge of the track. You need great **skill** and **bravery** to go fast on a street circuit without hitting the wall.

Azerbaijan is a small country on the border between Europe and Asia. It is located just below Russia and sits by the Caspian Sea. Baku is the capital city.

The country is so small, you could fit twenty Azerbaijans inside Greater London!

The **3.7-mile (6 km)** circuit is a fantastic mix of **superfast straights** and really **narrow stretches** where the track runs through the old, historic area of Baku.

F1 cars can reach more than **230 mph (370 kmh)** on the **1.25-mile (2 km)** blast to the finish line.

But drivers also must thread their way past old buildings where the track is only **25 feet (7.6 metres)** wide. Go too fast and cars will hit the concrete barriers protecting the ancient stone structures.

The Grands Prix in Baku have been **spectacular.**

Max Verstappen had a big crash in 2021 when his Red Bull suffered a puncture at 200 mph (322 kmh). Verstappen was thankfully unhurt.

Verstappen was also involved in a collision with **Daniel Ricciardo,** his Red Bull teammate in 2018. It took them both out of the race.

In 2017, **Sebastian Vettel** was penalized for

dangerous driving after swerving his Ferrari into Lewis Hamilton's Mercedes during the 2017 Grand Prix.

> Lewis Hamilton, Daniel Ricciardo and Max Verstappen – all Racing Legends – have won the Azerbaijan Grand Prix.

Leclerc loves street races. That's why the track at Baku is a favourite, along with Monaco.

Charles may have made a small mistake at Monaco when trying to improve his pole position time. But he was perfect in Baku.

This was his **ninth pole position!** He was determined to enjoy it because Charles knew the Mercedes and Red Bulls would be faster during the race.

And that's what happened. He held the lead for as long as he could but, one by one, his faster rivals got by. Charles finished fourth.

He was pleased with that.

He struggled to make the Ferrari fast enough in the next few races.

Then he got to **Silverstone** and the British Grand Prix.

There was the usual battle at the front between Lewis Hamilton's Mercedes and the Red Bull of Max Verstappen. But when these two collided on the first lap, Charles took the lead!

He stayed there until near the end. Then, with just three laps to go, Hamilton finally got by and won the race.

But Charles and Ferrari were very happy with **second place.**

That would be Leclerc's best result of the season. He finished **seventh in the World Championship.** This was an improvement on 2020.

2022 had to be *even* better!

BAHRAIN AGAIN

The 2022 Ferrari felt brilliant from the first moment Charles Leclerc drove the new red car. It was **more powerful** and felt nice to drive.

Charles was looking forward to the first race of 2022. This would be in **Bahrain.**

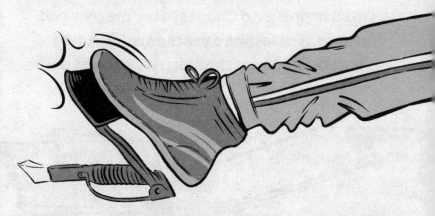

Charles had been on pole position in Bahrain in 2019. He finished third in that race.

Could he do better this time? The answer was 'Yes!'

From the moment the starting lights went out, he **led every lap** (except for a couple laps when he made a planned pit stop for new tyres).

No one could catch him. Not even Carlos Sainz in the other Ferrari. Or Max Verstappen, the new World Champion in his Red Bull.

Just for good measure, Charles set the **fastest lap** in the race. Having the fastest lap was worth another championship point!

'I'm so happy,' said Charles after the race had finished. 'The last two years have been very difficult. But, from the start, we knew this was

going to be a big opportunity for the team. The guys have done an incredible job building this amazing car. It's incredible to be back at the top!'

Everyone was saying Charles Leclerc could be World Champion in 2022.

But there were twenty-one more races. Charles knew there was a long way to go and anything could happen.

ON TOP DOWN UNDER

Leclerc finished **second** at the next race in **Saudi Arabia.**

The third race of 2022 was on the far side of the world.

The Australian Grand Prix is held in **Albert Park.** It is a popular race. The Australian fans can travel by tram from the centre of Melbourne to the race track. Albert Park is in a beautiful setting on the edge of the city. The track, which runs around a lake, is **3.2 miles (5.3 km)** long.

The Ferrari was the fastest car. Leclerc won pole position. He set the **fastest lap** of the race as he **led from start to finish.** This was a brilliant performance. He could not have done more.

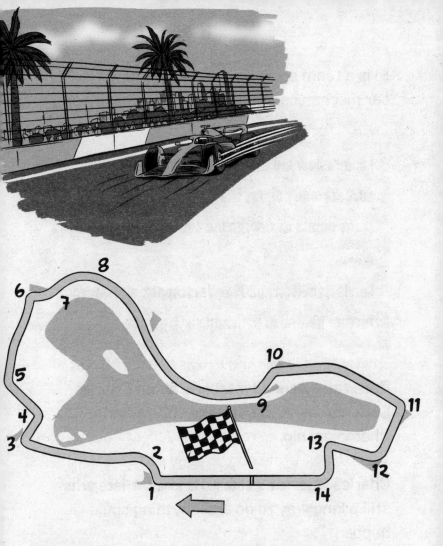

'What a car I had today!' said Charles, just
after the race had finished. 'I did a good job all
weekend, but it was not possible without the
car. Everything felt great from the first lap to
the last lap!'

131

F1 is a team sport, and winning is down to the car mechanics as much as it is to the drivers!

Leclerc now led the World Championship with seventy-one points. That was almost twice as many points as George Russell, who was in second place.

Lewis Hamilton and Max Verstappen were even further behind in fifth and sixth places.

Race fans were now talking about Charles Leclerc maybe winning the 2022 World Championship.

Charles was not so sure. He knew there was still a long way to go and anything could happen.

'It's only the third race,' said Charles. 'But we have a very good car. It's reliable, too.'

THE HOME OF FERRARI

The next race was in Italy. The home of Ferrari!

The **Imola circuit** is not far from the Ferrari factory in **Maranello.** Leclerc was leading the Drivers' World Championship. The passionate Ferrari fans – the Tifosi – came to Imola in their thousands expecting another win. There were red flags everywhere!

The excitement got too much for Leclerc. He had a **spin** during qualifying while fighting for pole position.

Max Verstappen started from pole. Charles was alongside the Red Bull on the front row of the grid.

Leclerc made a **bad start.** He was fourth by the end of the first lap.

Soon he was third and looking to take second place.

Then he had another spin! He didn't hit anything but the spin cost him precious time.

Charles was very disappointed to finish **sixth.** But he was still leading the championship!

A TOUGH TIME

Leclerc won pole position at the next two races. He finished second in **Miami** in the United States. That was good!

But then his Ferrari **broke** while he was leading in Spain. Now Max Verstappen snatched first place in the World Championship. This was not so good!

Never mind; **Monaco** was next! Charles's favourite race.

He won pole position yet again. Brilliant! This would be great for the Grand Prix.

Leclerc took the lead at the start. Carlos Sainz was behind Charles in the other Ferrari. The track was **wet** but they pulled away from everyone else. This was looking good!

Then the track began to dry. When would be a good time to have Leclerc and Sainz change from wet-weather tyres to slicks (dry-weather tyres)?

There was confusion at Ferrari. They made a pit stop for Leclerc at the wrong moment. Charles suddenly found himself in fourth place, behind two Red Bulls and Sainz.

This was a disaster for Leclerc! Now he was even further behind Verstappen in the World Championship after Max finished third in Monaco.

This was yet more disappointment for Leclerc at Monaco.

Leclerc would win just one more Grand Prix in 2022. That was in Austria.

He won an amazing nine pole positions and led many races.

There was one moment of Charles Leclerc

magic that the race fans would never forget.

This was during the British Grand Prix at Silverstone.

Leclerc was fighting for third place with Lewis Hamilton. Charles overtook Lewis by **going round the outside** of the Mercedes as they went through Copse Corner. At **180 mph (290 kmh)!**

It was INCREDIBLE! The crowd were on their feet. They couldn't believe Leclerc had done that. Nor could Lewis!

Leclerc finished **second in the World Championship.** Max Verstappen was champion again.

Would Leclerc do it in 2023?

2023 SEASON

The 2023 Grand Prix season was a tough test for Charles Leclerc.

Ferrari tried to make his car **faster.** Instead, they made it **more difficult** to drive.

Charles was brilliant during qualifying. He won five more pole positions. Only Max Verstappen, who would become 2023 World Champion, won more.

And yet Charles did not win a single race!

Ferrari won just one race in 2023. That was in Singapore and it was won by Carlos Sainz with Leclerc supporting his teammate for much of the race.

Charles led races on many occasions. But

140

things would go wrong. He would sometimes spin off because the car was difficult to drive.

Or the Ferrari would break down.

The **Brazilian Grand Prix** was very annoying for Leclerc. He had done a fantastic job by coming second in qualifying.

Then – unbelievably – the Ferrari went wrong just after Charles left the pits on his way to the starting grid. He never got to start the race!

How frustrating is that? Travel all the way to South America and not get to race!

Leclerc finished fifth in the drivers' 2023 World Championship. Sainz was seventh.

'We knew it would be a difficult year,' said Charles. 'I did my best. I want to thank the team. They never stopped trying to make things better. We will put everything we learned to good use. We want to give

141

something back to our fans for all their support.'

Leclerc and Sainz were making a very **good team** together. They got on well. This made life easy for everyone on the team.

Laurent Mekies, Ferrari's Sporting Director at the time, said: 'This partnership between Charles and Carlos is as good as it gets. It is deeper than being friends. There is respect and a desire to work together. The level of **trust** is huge.'

You don't often hear F1 bosses say that about their drivers! The drivers usually want to beat each other – no matter what it takes!

ALBERTO ASCARI

Alberto Ascari was from Italy. His father was a racing driver and won the Belgian Grand Prix.

In **1952,** Alberto became **Ferrari's first World Champion.**

Ascari won the championship again for Ferrari in **1953.**

He only took part in thirty-two Grands Prix – but he won **thirteen** of them! That's an amazing record.

Between 1952 and 1953, Ascari **won nine races in a row.** That was unheard of.

It would take many years before that record would be broken.

The Ascari family were born to race. They even have car in their surname!

There were fewer Grands Prix during the time when Ascari raced.

In 1952 there were only seven races. In 2024, there are twenty-four Grands Prix! That's three times as many.

Ascari liked to wear the same light blue crash helmet.

Ascari was very superstitious. He thought black cats were unlucky. If he saw a black cat in the street, he would turn his car around and drive in the opposite direction rather than pass the black cat!

Motor racing was very dangerous in the 1950s.

While leading the **1955 Monaco Grand Prix,** Ascari lost control of his car while leading, crashed into the harbour and disappeared beneath the water.

Amazingly, Ascari bobbed up to the surface and was rescued. They had to send divers down and hoist his car from the harbour by crane.

Four days later, Ascari died when practising in a Ferrari sports car at Monza, the race track not far from where he lived in the city of Milan.

Italy was heartbroken at the loss of their greatest champion. Thousands of people lined the streets for Ascari's funeral.

A FAST FRIEND

Charles Leclerc says **Pierre Gasly** is his best friend among the nineteen other Formula 1 drivers.

Although Pierre grew up in northern France, he met Charles when, aged seven and eight, they raced in the same karting events.

Their parents became good friends. They even went on holiday together!

Pierre remembers going to the Leclerc family's home in Monaco and hearing the exciting sound of Formula 1 cars on a Grand Prix weekend.

When he was fourteen, Pierre won the **French karting championship in 2010**. His teammate was Charles, who was thirteen. Charles was runner-up in the same championship.

'It was a really good fight between us for the championship,' says Pierre. 'We had a good time racing together. Although I moved into car racing before Charles, we kept a close friendship.'

Racing against each other in Formula 1 does not affect their friendship.

But their relationship was tested on the first lap of the **2021 Styrian Grand Prix** in Austria. The **front wing** of Leclerc's Ferrari **punctured** a rear tyre on Gasly's **AlphaTauri** as they fought for position.

Gasly was furious. It meant he had to retire. But he knew it had not been a deliberate move by Leclerc. Both drivers spoke after the race. All was well between them.

'Yes, of course we are trying to beat each other on the track!' says Charles. 'That's what we've always done, right from when we were karting when we were very young. But that does not affect our friendship away from the track.'

When the 2023 Chinese Grand Prix was cancelled at the last minute, the F1 drivers had a free weekend. Charles and Pierre went together to watch the Monaco Masters tennis final. They both enjoy sports of all kinds.

ON TREND

Charles Leclerc's career goes beyond just racing. His good looks caught the attention of a major Italian fashion company.

Giorgio Armani use Leclerc to **model** their smart suits.

His fashion shoots are probably the only times Charles has worn a tie!

Lewis Hamilton also likes to show off nice clothes for **Tommy Hilfiger.**

Charles is an ambassador for the Princess Charlene of Monaco Foundation. This is a charity that encourages people – particularly children - to **learn to swim.**

151

During the Covid-19 crisis in 2020, Charles was happy to work with the Monaco **Red Cross.** He drove a van delivering urgent medical supplies to elderly people who could not leave their homes because of Covid.

He drove that white van much, MUCH slower than he drives the red Ferrari Formula 1 car around the same streets of his home town!

Charles learned to **play the piano** when he was little.

He finds playing the piano a nice way to **relax** after returning home from a busy weekend at a Grand Prix.

Charles took lessons and played the piano a lot when stuck at home in Monaco during Covid-19. He became really good – and enjoyed playing the piano even more.

Charles's white piano had to be lifted by crane to get into his apartment in Monaco!

Charles wrote a tune. It was called 'AUS23 (1:1)'. It was an immediate hit on Spotify.

It is very different from the usual sound Charles hears when racing – the **roar** of a Ferrari engine!

RACING IN STYLE

Charles Leclerc is one of the **fastest** drivers in Formula 1.

He is also one of the most **spectacular** – which is why fans love to watch him.

Charles likes the car to **slide** when he goes into a corner.

This is a very fast way to take the corner. But it is also **risky.**

If Leclerc makes the car slide too much, he will spin off. This has happened occasionally.

But most of the time, Charles keeps the Ferrari **under control** and is unbelievably fast.

This is why he has won so many pole positions.

155

Nobody can go as fast as Charles when he is happy with his car and in total control.

That's why the guy in Ferrari number 16 is always brilliant to watch!

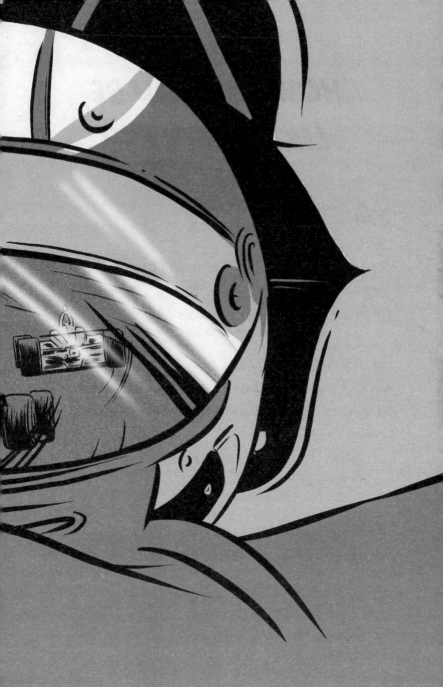

HOW CAN YOU BE LIKE CHARLES?

Charles started his racing in karts.

Most of the drivers in Formula 1 began that way when they were very young. Some were only four or five years old!

There are thousands of race tracks around the world. You will find a motor race somewhere on any weekend outside the winter season.

In the UK, there are more than forty motor racing tracks!

The biggest and best in England are **SILVERSTONE** and **BRANDS HATCH.**

You can also go to smaller tracks where it is easier to move around and see the cars and drivers up close.

These are fun events. This sort of racing is known as CLUB RACING.

There is not the pressure of big race meetings like Grands Prix.

You can watch the racing live and see how exciting it is!

Here are some great places to watch club racing in the UK:

WALES

PEMBREY Carmarthenshire

ANGLESEY Anglesey

SCOTLAND

INGLISTON Edinburgh

KNOCKHILL Fife

ENGLAND

THRUXTON Hampshire

BRANDS HATCH Kent

CASTLE COMBE Wiltshire

SNETTERTON Norfolk

SILVERSTONE Northamptonshire

MALLORY PARK Leicestershire

DONINGTON PARK East Midlands

OULTON PARK Cheshire

CADWELL PARK Lincolnshire

CROFT North Yorkshire

NORTHERN IRELAND

KIRKISTOWN County Down

BISHOPSCOURT County Down

ABOUT THE AUTHOR

Maurice Hamilton, the award-winning author of more than **thirty books** about motor sport, has attended over **500 Grands Prix** around the world. He has been a commentator on F1 races for BBC Radio 5 Live for **twenty years,** and has written about F1 for newspapers and magazines **worldwide** for decades.

ABOUT THE ILLUSTRATOR

Combining her love of **comics** with a passion for **social equality, Cat Sims** has pursued her dream career as an **artist** and **illustrator** for the past decade. She has worked on a huge range of commercial and personal projects for clients including *The New Yorker*, *Jacobin*, Adidas, the BBC and many more.
www.catsims.org / @cat_sims

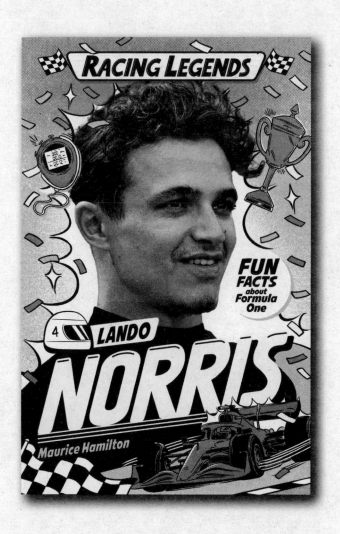

**MORE
RACING LEGENDS
COMING SOON IN
JANUARY 2025!**